Unbelievable Pictures and Facts About Papua New Guinea

By: Olivia Greenwood

Introduction

Many people have never heard of a county called Papua New Guinea. If you are one of them not to worry, as we will be introducing you to this very interesting country right here right now. Prepare to learn some new and wonderful things about this mysterious country.

Where in the world is Papua New Guinea situated?

Papua New Guinea is situated on the continent that is called Oceania. If you have trouble finding it then all you need to do is look for some of the places that it is bordered by. You can look for the Pacific Ocean, Solomon Sea, or even Indonesia on the west side.

What type of landscape does the country have?

Papua New Guinea has a really beautiful landscape that consists of mountains, tropical rainforests, and even coral reefs.

Are there many different bird species in the country?

The country is a real treat for people who love birds. Did you know that some people try to find and identify different birds as a hobby? This is called birdwatching and Papua New Guinea is the perfect place for birdwatching as there are over seven hundred and fifty different types of birds.

Do we know what their official national sport is?

The official national sport of Papua New Guinea is rugby.

What year did Papua New Guinea gain independence from Australia?

We do know what year Papua New Guinea gained independence from Australia and this was in 1975.

Is Papua New Guinea considered to be a very explored place?

The answer is a big no, Papua New Guinea is considered to be one of the most unexplored places in the entire world.

Is there anything unique about the languages that people speak?

There is something very unique with the languages that people speak in the country. The country is known worldwide for having the most diverse spoken languages on the planet. There are over eight hundred different languages spoken in Papua New Guinea.

Is Papua New Guinea a big country or a small country?

In terms of size, the country is relatively big as it is the fifty-fourth biggest country in the world. It is also known to be the third biggest island country in the whole world, which is very impressive.

Do we know the specific name of the capital city?

The name of the capital city is a name you more than likely have never heard of before. It is called Port Moresby and it is also the biggest city that exists in Papua New Guinea.

What are some of the main towns in the country?

Some of the main towns in this special island country consist of Lae, Rabaul, Madang, Wewak, and of course the capital Port Moresby.

Is visiting Papua New Guinea safe or not?

Unfortunately, the truth is that Papua New Guinea is not a safe place to visit. Many violent crimes and all sorts of bad things take place in the country.

What are some of the main products that Papua New Guinea exports?

The things that Papua New Guinea is known for exporting include copper, gold, palm oil, and even coffee.

Do the people in Papua New Guinea have regular access to clean water?

Unfortunately, Papua New Guinea has the least access to clean water out of every place in the entire world. Many people live without clean water and this is quite normal in certain areas. Some people make use of dirty water and they get extremely sick. Sometimes the water runs dry and they have no access to water at all not even to wash with.

Will you find many markets in Papua New Guinea?

If you enjoy shopping, you will be glad to know that there are many markets situated all over Papua New Guinea. However there are not many shopping malls, so you will have to replace your usual shopping experience with these fun markets.

Do people live in poverty in Papua New Guinea?

Unfortunately, the sad truth is that many people in Papua New Guinea live in extreme levels of poverty.

Do many different ethnic groups live in Papua New Guinea?

Believe it or not, there are more than one thousand different ethnic groups in Papua New Guinea. This island country is filled with all kinds of different people.

What financial currency do they use in Papua New Guinea?

If you ever find yourself in Papua New Guinea you will need to use their currency to buy things. The specific currency that they use is called Papua New Guinean Kina.

Are all the areas in Papua New Guinea geared for tourists?

The answer is a big no, many areas in Papua New Guinea are very undeveloped. The rural areas have no modern facilities at all, which are far from tourist-friendly areas.

Is it expensive to travel and do things in Papua New Guinea?

The answer is yes, things like accommodation in Papua New Guinea tend to cost lots of money especially for tourists.

What is the average lifespan in Papua New Guinea?

For a country that may be behind in many aspects, life expectancy is not bad at all. The average age that people live up until is over the age of sixty-five.